DAVID
Israel's Shepherd-King

John C. Ibisch

NORTHWESTERN PUBLISHING HOUSE
Milwaukee, Wisconsin

To my parents and my wife for their
nurturing, enabling, and prayers.

Second edition, 2014

Cover illustration: Johnson and Fancher
Interior illustrations: Samantha Burton, Frank Ordaz

Northwestern Publishing House
1250 N. 113th St., Milwaukee, WI 53226-3284
www.nph.net
© 2005 Northwestern Publishing House
Published 2005
Printed in China
ISBN 978-0-8100-1338-4

CONTENTS

They have been referred to as the saints, the Hebrews, the Israelites, a remnant, and the church. They are God's people—his *chosen* people. They belong to him; so precious that he would go to impossible lengths to overcome the gulf that separates them from himself. You and I are among them.

The books in this series are a recital of the life and times of some of them—Noah, Jacob, Ruth, David, Jonah, Paul, and others. Their stories involve conflict and resolution, pain and tragedy, despondency and renewal. They present disturbing images from the underbelly of human depravity, and visions of untold glory that transport us to the soaring heights of ultimate conquest. The plots and settings are drawn from the living record of the Bible. Series authors and editors were careful to remain faithful to that record. Yet today's sophisticated reading audiences demand background and description. They relate to narrative. In an effort to make the text come alive, each story in this series is presented in a natural framework designed for this audience.

In these stories we see God's people wrestling with their humanity and struggling to find respite for their souls. Each story is unique in its own right. Yet two common threads run through the fabric of their stories and ours. The first is the thread of the bitter curse of sin. The second is the golden thread of salvation in Christ Jesus. We can readily identify with both, for we share these same two themes with all of God's people. Their stories, like ours, rest forever in God's abiding grace.

Kenneth Kremer, Series Editor

As the hot sun burned off the morning dew, the teen stared at what would be his day's work—a flock of bleating sheep. A sheepherder's daily routine could be mind numbing. David allowed his thoughts to drift to more important matters, like the age-old questions all teenagers ask sooner or later: *Where do I fit in?* and *Why am I here?*

David knew his history well. He was a descendant of Abraham's grandson Jacob, living in what we know as modern Israel. Until 1000 B.C., the nation of God's chosen people had been a theocracy. Through a succession of judges, God himself had governed it. But that was then; now there was a new way of ruling. God's people had demanded a king. They wanted a monarchy—a government more like that of the other nations of their day. A man named Saul had been Israel's king as long as young David could remember. And now, as David thought about his nation's future, the questions loomed even more personal: *So what does the future hold for me, a poor shepherd boy?*

The same bright dawn had awakened Samuel, the last of the prophet-judges of Israel. Samuel also found himself deep in thought. Under his predecessor, the Israelites' trust in God had eroded. Many of the people had come to place their faith in objects, like the ark of the covenant, rather than in God himself. The people had treated the ark like a lucky charm. The "lucky" ark had even been carried into battle when the Israelites fought their perennial enemies on the Mediterranean seacoast, the Philistines. That very day the Philistines had killed many of Israel's brave soldiers, and the enemy had carried off the ark. That was the same day that Samuel's predecessor had died and

ISRAEL'S SHEPHERD-KING

Samuel had become the new prophet-judge in Israel.

But God had not died. The power of the Lord, the God of Israel, still exhibited itself. Whenever the Philistines had left the ark in the presence of their idols, the idols fell on their faces, losing hands and heads. Also, the Philistine people had begun to suffer from a dreadful affliction, something akin to bubonic plague. So Israel's enemies temporarily sued for peace, sending the ark of the covenant back into Israelite territory along with a peace offering of gold "tumors," reflective of the enlarged lymph nodes that the disease caused, and gold mice, because the land had been overrun with the vermin.

That was how Samuel's judgeship had begun, blessed with an uneasy peace.

Israel Demands a King

Samuel served faithfully. He lived as God's handpicked representative and spokesman. But as time passed, God's powerful plague was forgotten, among both the Philistines and God's people.

New military threats appeared on the horizon. But the people of Israel did not take their concerns to God. They decided to do whatever they thought was best, without consulting God through their prophet-judge. When they did come to Samuel, it was with more of a demand than a cry for God's help: "Give us a king!"

Samuel was devastated by their rejection. But God had to correct his prophet. "They have not rejected you. They have rejected me," he said. "Go, and give them their king!"

Samuel followed God's direction and anointed the reluctant Saul, son of Kish, from the tribe of Benjamin. Saul was declared king of all Israel.

Things changed under Saul, at least militarily. No longer did an Israelite army, armed with clubs and farming tools, come together for doing battle in God's name. Starting with only two swords, King Saul quickly raised a standing army of no less than three thousand men. David's oldest brothers were attracted to that service. Successive, God-given victories equipped Israel's army with the iron weapons of the defeated Philistines and enriched Israel's people with plunder.

A Disappointing Record

But God was not pleased. "Saul, Saul, Saul, where did you go wrong?" Samuel cried, tears welling in his eyes. The king who had begun his reign in such humility had not remained faithful to God. Instead of obeying God and trusting him to carry out his will in his own time and way, Saul now chose to rule independently. He dared to disobey God's direct command, which was brought to him by Samuel. Now Samuel's heart ached as he remembered the admonition he had spoken to Saul: "To obey is better than to sacrifice." Hot tears wet Samuel's cheeks as he remembered his pronouncement: "God has rejected you, Saul, as king of Israel!" It was a bitter moment, for Samuel loved Saul!

This was to be David's world. And even as these events were transpiring, David, the shepherd boy, wondered, *Where do I fit in?*

ISRAEL'S SHEPHERD-KING

Samuel's mourning over Saul's failures had finally ended when God spoke to the grieving prophet-judge: "How long will you mourn for Saul, since I have rejected him as king over Israel? Fill your horn with oil and be on your way. I am sending you to Jesse of Bethlehem. I have chosen one of his sons to be king."

Samuel was slow to obey. His heart was filled with its own fears. *How can I go? Saul will hear about it and kill me.* (Even prophets struggle with weakness and doubt. But the Lord God always has a way.)

"Take a heifer with you," God said. "Say, 'I have come to sacrifice to the LORD.' Invite Jesse to the sacrifice. You are to anoint for me the one I indicate."

Obediently, Samuel set out on his journey. He headed south toward the hills of Bethlehem. There he would do the Lord's bidding, unaware that a thousand years later those same hills would be populated by shepherds seeking an infant, a royal descendant of the young shepherd named David.

First one. Then two. Soon the meadow was filled with the morning calls of the bulbul, lark, collared dove, and warblers. These gentle sounds roused David as he laid akimbo, his body stretched across the gate of the sheepfold. It was a personal way to keep his flock safe inside the bramble barrier overnight. Any predators lurking outside the barrier would have to negotiate their way past him to get to his flock.

God had brought the Israelites to a land flowing with milk and honey. Yet over the years, wars and foreign invasions had decimated the areas around the towns. Trees had been cut down and burned for fuel or used to build siege equipment and bulwarks. But in the fields and on the hillsides, the grass and flowers, the lilies and anemones, the oaks, terebinths, and acacias still reflected the rich bounty of the land into which God had brought his people.

The youngest of Jesse of Bethlehem's sons opened his eyes upon the morning star, the planet Venus, which heralded the arrival of the dawn. He exulted, "I will praise you, for I am fearfully and wonderfully made!" The starry host was quickly fading from sight. "The heavens declare the glory of God!" David's heart filled with wonder and joy. He could not resist drawing his nine-stringed kinnor, his lyre, from its bag. The sheep choir was already beginning to lift its voice with "baa-a-a-a-as" of bass to treble timbre. Each sheep had a voice of its own. David recognized each one, just as well as each sheep recognized his voice. His calloused fingers plucked the strings and continued his song of praise: "The skies proclaim the work of your hands." Confronted by the witness of God's creation, touched by the Lord's love, songs of praise regularly tumbled from David's lips. It was a gift from the Almighty that he was able to put words and music together so artfully. Already at an early age, the young singer used his gift to sing of the glory of his Creator, even if his only audience was a flock of clueless animals.

A Young Shepherd's Preparation

Daily the young shepherd was awed by the very existence of his world and confronted with the fingerprints of God in the intricate design of nature. The physical realities of nature confirmed the creation account of the Scriptures—the books of Moses that David knew by heart. He sang again: "The law of the LORD is perfect, reviving the soul. The statutes of the LORD are trustworthy, making wise the simple. . . . May the words of my mouth and the meditation of my heart be pleasing in your sight, O LORD, my Rock and my Redeemer." Prayer closed his song and began his day. And then he thought once more, *Where do I fit in? What is God's plan for my life?*

When he was about 17 years old, David was shepherding his father's flock alone for the first time. He felt like a man. He now would have to decide when to move on to find greener pasture, gather the strays, lead them to water, or draw refreshing cistern water for them. The hill country of all of southern Judah was becoming familiar to the young shepherd.

David's LORD (*Yahweh*)
and David's God (*Elohim*)

The names LORD and God are picture names. David knew his God by both names.

The name LORD, which is *Yahweh* in Hebrew, is the personal name that presents God's essence. This name helps us see our God as a God of rescue and deliverance. He identified himself with this name in the Garden of Eden when he promised to send a Savior to Adam and Eve. The LORD intervened over and over to save the people he loved. When we read the name LORD (in all capital letters) in the Old Testament today, we think of our loving Savior-Friend.

Elohim, a plural Hebrew form, describes God's creative, preserving power as well as the amazing fact that he is three persons yet one God. The name depicts God's limitless power and knowledge. For David this name for God pictured the awesome Triune-Creator-Preserver-Ruler. "God" should have the same meaning for us every time we see it in our Bibles, hear it in church, or use it in our conversations.

But it was always good to be close to home. Nothing seemed to compare to the beauty of Bethlehem's skies at nightfall.

Whooooosh, whooosh, whoosh—ka-ching! The stone glanced off the side of the boulder. David had intended it to hit dead center. The sheep had been watered. David had daubed their noses with a sticky pitch, which protected them from the stinging botflies. They were resting quietly in the shade of the acacia trees on the hillside, and David was practicing. He had seen the skills with a sling that the shepherds of Benjamin possessed. He was determined to someday command the same expertise. A shepherd's club, or rod, and crooked staff were fine for close work; but if a shepherd could hit a marauding lion or a bear with a half-pound stone traveling at 150 mph, one might not have to do any close work. David placed another stone in his sling and swung it around his head. This time it missed the boulder entirely. Patience! Practice!

As the afternoon wore on, the shadow of an occasional cloud swept across the landscape. Once when the bright sun shone on the distant road from Jebus to Bethlehem, it revealed the figure of an old man driving a heifer.

Anointing Israel's Future King

The break between Saul and Samuel had become well known. Leaders of all the tribes had been present when King Saul had disobeyed God's direct command and spared the life of the Amalekite king. All of Israel had heard the story of how Samuel had borrowed a sword and, obeying the command of God, slew the enemy leader in the presence of King Saul

A SHEPHERD'S PROMOTION

himself. Now word had preceded the prophet, and a gaggle of Bethlehem's anxious elders greeted the craggy-visaged prophet with a question, "Do you come in peace?"

"Yes, in peace; I have come to sacrifice to the LORD. Consecrate yourselves and come to the sacrifice."

Samuel's mission to anoint the next king of Israel was not mentioned. Jesse and all but one of his sons were invited. Before the sacrifice, the prophet was introduced to Jesse's seven grown sons—impressive men! Samuel, who had been awed with King Saul's stature, thought, "Surely the LORD's anointed stands here!" But as physically impressive as the young men were, Samuel heard God say: "I do not look at the things man looks at. . . . The LORD looks at the heart."

None of Jesse's seven sons was God's choice. Could there be another? Yes, but he was just a boy, hardly fit to do anything more than tend the needs of his father's sheep. But, yes, he could be called.

The sacrifice waited while a servant ran to the distant flock to replace David, who, in turn, quickly made his way back to Bethlehem. Flushed from his run, David's naturally ruddy good looks seemed to shine.

"Rise and anoint him; he is the one" was God's direction.

Pure olive oil ran through David's curly chestnut hair, trickled over his beardless face, and ran down onto his clothes. His family stood in awed silence. Who had even thought for a moment to consider the youngest brother, David, as Israel's future monarch? As one stalwart brother after another stepped before Samuel, fatherly pride prompted Jesse to think over and over, "My son!" But it was to be none of them. Rather David—the shepherd boy, the singer of songs, the one who annoyed his brothers with his pious words and public confessions—was God's choice as the next king of Israel.

Caring for His Father's Flock

But as the solemn ceremony drew to a close, some were left to wonder. Was Jesse not suitably impressed or was he just a wise father? Because after the sacrifice was completed and Samuel had returned home, the newly anointed king of Israel was sent back to the fields from which he had been called. And there, in the hills overlooking the little village of Bethlehem, David continued to mature as a man after the Lord's own heart.

God's ways are not man's ways, and the experiences David had with his flock served to bring him into a close, prayer-filled relationship with his Lord. Because the shepherd's life is one of constant service to his flock, the Judean hillsides provided a good field for training the great shepherd-king of Israel. The shepherd had to lead his flock to pasture and water, provide escape from the flies, seek the straying and the lost lambs, protect one and all—by day with his sling and rod, by night with his body blocking the gate of the sheepfold.

David's calloused fingers picked out a melody, and his song comforted the woolly choir as it quieted down for the night: "The LORD is my shepherd, I shall not be in want. . . . I will fear no evil. . . . Your rod and your staff, they comfort me." The Spirit of the Lord was upon him, and David slept as peacefully as his flock.

Time passed, and the young shepherd continued to care for, move, feed, and protect his wayward flock. David's anointing slowly faded from the memories of the handful of people who knew about it. His questions, *Where do I fit in?* and *Why am I here?* still seemed to have no answers. But God would soon open another chapter in David's life.

King Saul's days and nights were not peaceful. Having turned away from God, Saul was afflicted with an evil spirit that pushed him toward despondency and despair. As Saul drifted in and out of depression, his servants suggested that he try the healing power of music. One servant had heard David play. He knew of David's reputation as a fine singer. Saul ordered Jesse, "Send me your son, David, the boy who is tending your sheep."

The young man's music and spiritual songs soon pleased the king. For the sake of the public record, David officially entered into the king's service as an armor-bearer. In reality, he was on call day and night to minister to a suffering king with his music. Through this service, God had arranged for David to learn how Israel's royal court functioned. It was on-site training for the young, future king. And the king's part-time armor-bearer would also learn how to use sword and spear. Still, David kept silent regarding his anointing. It was not wise to speak about that in the politically charged environment of Saul's court. So while David was often heard singing, he remained almost invisible.

A Shepherd's Courage

Saul's condition improved. Soon David was allowed to return to Bethlehem. There, as a lowly shepherd, David was among the least in society. But he was growing to manhood. A soft beard and maturing body began to display the physical gifts that Samuel had admired in Jesse's older sons. When a lion and a bear attacked the flock, David killed both with his shepherd's rod and sling.

A test of courage had also come for the three eldest sons of Jesse as they served in Saul's standing army. Battle lines separating Israel's army from the Philistines had been drawn in the Valley of Elah. For 40 days the armies postured without fighting. Much of the ugly business of war is psychological, and the opposing forces were evenly matched, except for one man. The man was not Saul, now over 60 years old and still a head taller than other Israelites. Saul kept to his tent. No, the man of the hour was Goliath the Gittite!

Modern warfare can appear to be antiseptic. Air strikes, missiles, and long-range guns produce carnage and death, but the soldier who inflicts the destruction may never see a person actually killed. In the Judean hill country, where chariots had a difficult time negotiating the hilly field of battle, warfare was very personal—man-on-man.

In a one-on-one fight, the odds were clearly in Goliath's favor. He stood nearly 10 feet tall, and his armor and weaponry were unmatched by Israel's protective battle armor and armaments. Courage was one thing; but it would require something more like a death wish to stand up against this giant.

For 40 days Goliath strode forth, issuing a challenge. "Why line up for battle? Choose a champion!" Seven-foot King Saul cowered in his tent, wisely ignoring the invitation to engage in man-to-man combat as the Philistine ridiculed the men of Israel and blasphemed their God. "Choose a champion. If he kills me, we will become your subjects. If I kill him, you will become our slaves and serve us."

A Life-or-Death Decision

As David arrived in camp with food supplies sent from Jesse for his eldest sons, no one noticed him. All eyes were riveted on Goliath across the valley. And David too heard Goliath's challenge: "This day I defy the ranks of Israel! Give me a man and let us fight each other!"

No man in Israel stepped forward, not even after Saul promised to give his daughter in marriage, great wealth, and a tax exemption to any man who would kill Goliath. Instead, the ranks nearest the giant scurried back up the hill to safer ground.

Hearing Goliath's challenge and blasphemy, pious David was incensed. "Who is this uncircumcised Philistine that he should defy the armies of the living God?" He went from group to group expressing his dismay at Israel's cowardice. Were the men of Israel all hypocrites?

Overhearing David's comments and questions, the angry feelings of his eldest brother surfaced: "Why have you come down here? And with whom did you leave our father's sheep out in the desert? I know how conceited you are and how wicked your heart is; you came down only to watch the battle."

At this rebuke, David held his tongue. Even though he was a young man in his early 20s, he was still a child in his brother's eyes.

"Can't I even speak?" asked David. His brother's stinging rejection had hurt. But David's rejection here foreshadowed the rejection that the future Shepherd-King, also hailing from Bethlehem, would experience from his own spiritual brethren.

By this time David's words had reached King Saul. Could it be that there was one soldier in the ranks willing to fight Goliath?

David obeyed the king's summons. Saul, the grizzled warrior, eyed the young man. Initially, he saw nothing but a lowly shepherd in his dirty robes.

David spoke first: "Let no one lose heart on account of this Philistine; your servant will go and fight him."

Sixty-year-old Saul did not recognize the speaker: "You are only a boy, and Goliath has been a fighting man from his youth."

Then the Spirit of God filled David. He recounted his physical battles in the fields with the lion and bear, killing both with nothing but his shepherd's rod. "This uncircumcised Philistine will be like one of them, because he has defied the armies of the living God. The LORD will deliver me from the hand of this Philistine." David knew his God was the Lord, the God of rescue and deliverance!

Saul was impressed. The shepherd under the robes

Goliath the Gittite

Goliath was about 9'5" tall, not counting the massive brass Philistine helmet on his head. What an intimidating champion! Wearing 125 pounds of polished bronze scales of body armor, Goliath appeared invincible. His legs were protected with bronze greaves and his armor-bearer carried a full-length body shield in front of him. For close fighting he had a sword; he was also equipped with the missile of the day, a bronze javelin strapped to his back, and a massive spear with an iron point that weighed 15 pounds. He was the impregnable tank of his day. Many of Saul's soldiers did not even possess iron weapons.

was not a boy at all but a hardened man, grown enough to consider being armed with Saul's own coat of mail and his own bronze helmet.

Saul ordered David to lay aside his shepherd's cloak and mantle and to put on the king's own personal armor; David obeyed. Then David buckled the sword at his waist and tried walking around to get used to the armor.

Saul was impressed and pleased with what he saw: "Go, and the LORD be with you."

But David surprised him: "I cannot go into battle like this because I am not used to this armor." It had been too long since the young armor-bearer's experience. This battle outfit was too large, too bulky, too heavy. David knew instinctively that he would not be able to move quickly and effectively. So David took off all the armor that Saul had offered. Instead, wearing only his knee-length tunic with his staff in one hand and his sling in the other, David left Saul and headed straight for the Israelite lines to begin his descent to the valley floor below. Approaching the stream that flowed there, he stopped and carefully chose five smooth stones, each the size of a child's fist. These he put into his shepherd's bag.

Face-to-Face with the Enemy

Goliath was insulted. Dressed only in his sleeveless under-garment, David appeared naked before the massed lines of gleaming armored bodies. Almost 4 feet shorter than Goliath and equipped with only his lowly shepherd's gear, David steadily kept climbing up the valley's opposite slope toward the

DAVID AND GOLIATH

towering giant.

Goliath badly misread the situation. He saw David as nothing more than a shepherd boy, a child. "Am I a dog that you come at me with a stick?" shouted the enemy of God's people. Then Goliath tried to plant the seeds of doubt in David's mind by calling his attention to the giant buzzards with 10-foot wingspans, griffon vultures, which were circling above the valley. Calling on his false god, Dagon, Goliath cursed David: "Come here, and I'll give your flesh to the birds of the air and the beasts of the field."

The lines of soldiers on the opposing hillside expected the youth to waver, to recoil in fear. But David was fearless. His faith was on fire. "You come against me with sword and spear. I come against you in the name of the LORD Almighty, the God of the armies of Israel, whom you have defied. The LORD will hand you over to me. I'll strike you down and cut off your head! The whole world will know that there is a God in Israel. It is not by sword or spear that the LORD saves. The battle is the LORD's, and he will give all of you into our hands."

The distance between the two warriors closed as Goliath lumbered forward. The words of David's own song were never truer: "Even though I walk through the valley of the shadow of death, I will fear no evil, for you are with me." David had experienced the blessing of his Lord God in the fields. He knew the promise of his Lord God in Scripture. Empowered by a courageous faith in God, David pulled a stone from his bag and dropped it into the pocket of his sling. Whoooosh, whooosh, whoosh! The sling whistled in the air. "The battle is the LORD's!" David cried. Then he unleashed his stone missile.

The long, lonely hours of practice coupled with the Lord's guidance on that day caused the stone to crush the exposed frontal bone and sink deep into Goliath's forehead. The stunned armor-bearer watched as the invincible Philistine champion stumbled, pitched, and then fell headlong. The hushed silence of the valley was broken by the sound of Goliath's armor as he crashed to the ground.

A Decisive Victory

David's momentum carried him forward until he was on top of Goliath. He drew the fallen champion's sword from it massive sheath, and a moment later he raised Goliath's huge severed head before the two opposing armies.

The Philistines turned and fled.

The Israelites, galvanized by David's heroic victory, rushed after their retreating foes.

When the dust settled, Saul did not let David return to his father's house. Instead, from that day on, Saul kept David nearby. The sweet singer had returned to court. "The LORD is my light and my salvation—whom shall I fear? The LORD is the stronghold of my life—of whom shall I be afraid? When evil men advance against me to devour my flesh, when my enemies and my foes attack me, they will stumble and fall." The court of Saul echoed once again with the songs of David's faith-filled heart.

Where do I fit in? What does the future hold for me? David descended the hillside as a hero for the Israelites and a feared enemy for the Philistines. The shepherd boy descended the hillside a champion. Now he had honor, a position in Saul's army, and a new friend: Jonathan, the eldest son of King Saul.

The names of Saul's sons, Jonathan and Ishbaal, reflected the king's spiritual drift away from the Lord. His firstborn he had named Jonathan, which means "gift of God." But Saul gave his younger son Ishbaal a name that honored a pagan fertility god.

Jonathan was born into a home that had revered the Lord. He exhibited faith in the true God throughout his life. Seven years before David rallied Israel against Goliath, Jonathan had led a similar successful assault on the Philistines, crying, "Nothing can hinder the LORD from saving, whether by many or by few. Come up with me. The LORD has given them into our hands." A great victory had followed.

Perceiving in David a kindred spirit and the same confident faith in God's ability to save, Jonathan generously solved the problem of David's odd battle dress. He took off his own sword, belt, bow, royal robe, and fine linen tunic and gave them to David as a replacement for the dirty shepherd's tunic. The covenant of friendship they made that day would never be broken.

A Jealous King

Soon everyone in Israel knew about David's wisdom and courage. Everything Saul assigned to David was completed successfully. He was given a high rank in the army, which won the hearty approval of the officers and the regular soldiers alike. Israel now enjoyed a series of victories over the Philistines. Saul was pleased with his young commander.

But it didn't take long before Saul overheard a troubling refrain sung by the women who came out to greet Israel's returning army: "Saul has slain his thousands, and David his tens of thousands!" A canker of envy and jealousy replaced the joy in Saul's heart. Now he suddenly viewed David as a threat to his throne—a threat that had to be removed! So Saul's jealous eye began to watch the shepherd-turned-soldier, and his evil heart plotted David's death.

Saul's own treachery caused his evil spirit to return, more forceful than before. One day as David played his harp and sang, Saul grabbed his spear and said to himself, *I'll pin him to the wall.* He hurled it at David with all his strength . . . and missed.

Thank God for guardian angels and David's quick reflexes! Saul rushed across the room to retrieve the spear and threw it again, only to miss a second time. Now David knew that Saul had become his enemy.

A Dowry for the King's Daughter

Having failed in this personal attack, Saul decided to commission David as the commander of a thousand men. His plot had this intent: "I will not raise a hand against David. Let the Philistines do that!" But the Lord was with David, and all of the people of Israel and Judah loved him as he led them to victory after victory.

DAVID THE HERO

Popular opinion forced King Saul to keep his promise. He offered his eldest daughter to David in marriage. As the youngest son of his family, without wealth or inheritance, David humbly declined the honor of a royal marriage. "Who am I, and what is my family or my father's clan in Israel, that I should become the king's son-in-law?" Saul did not mind the polite refusal. He gave his eldest daughter's hand to another man who offered a rich dowry.

But royal marriage was not altogether out of the picture. Saul's younger daughter, Michal, had fallen in love with the ruddy good looks and gallant reputation of the young war hero. But it was the sensual images that Michal savored, not David's faith. She had her own idol images for private worship.

Saul, ever plotting, soon learned of Michal's infatuation. He decided, "I will give her to him so that she may be a snare to him and so that I may use the hand of the Philistines against him." Addressing David through his servants, Saul said, "Now you have a second opportunity to become my son-in-law." He instructed them to add these words as if they were their own: "Look, the king is pleased with you, and his attendants all like you; now become his son-in-law."

But David's common-sense response to the persuasive temptation again was this: "Do you think it is a small matter to become the king's son-in-law? I am only a poor man."

David's concern about the dowry had been part of Saul's plan all along. Aware of David's comments about the uncircumcised Goliath, a mark that set Israelite men apart from other nations, Saul set what he thought was a clever trap. "Say to David, 'The king wants no other price for the bride than a hundred Philistine foreskins, to take revenge on his enemies.'" Saul was confident that such an impossible mission would surely bring David to his death at the hands of the Philistines.

But it was just such a bloody dowry that a warrior like David could provide. Before the allotted time was up, David and his men returned with not one hundred but two hundred foreskins and presented the king with the gruesome price for his second daughter's hand.

With his terms met, Saul kept his promise and gave Michal to David in marriage. But the intimacy of wedded life that the lonely shepherd had dreamed of was almost nonexistent. It was interrupted by repeated calls to campaigns and battles in which David was consistently victorious. When David, the public hero, finally returned to court, Saul's hatred prompted him to make another attempt on David's life with the spear. David then fled to his home and wife.

Michal's Treachery

Knowing her father's hatred for David, Michal insisted that her husband leave the house under the cover of darkness. Following her directions, David was lowered from an upper window and fled into the night. Then Michal brought out her idol, put goat's hair at its head, and tucked it into David's bedclothes.

When Saul's soldiers discovered the ruse, Michal was taken to Saul. While being questioned by her angry father, she misrepresented David and his words. "He said to me, 'Help me get away, or I will kill you!'" The words she ascribed to David redirected her father's rage from herself back to her husband. They made David appear to be an evil man.

With David in disfavor and in hiding, Michal professed no love for him. Perhaps David had failed to live up to Michal's high expectations. Perhaps the openness of his faith in the true God had annoyed idolatrous Michal. Perhaps the continuous campaigns had kept them from forming the foundation for marriage that God had in mind when he made the rule that a man not be required to serve in the army for a full year after his marriage. In any case, Saul resolved the matter by giving Michal to another man who loved her.

Where do I fit in? Why am I here? What does the future hold for me? The questions of David's youth still haunted him. As a fugitive, his future as Israel's next king was hardly a sure thing.

David, the fugitive, fled to Samuel. Those unanswered questions seemed more appropriate than ever. He participated in the activities of the school of the aged prophet. He wrote Psalm 119: "Rulers persecute me without cause, but my heart trembles at your word. . . . I wait for your salvation, O Lord, and I follow your commands." To faithful people, God's Word is filled with promise and blessings. David's faith flourished in the atmosphere of the school. His words foreshadowed the perfect obedience of his future descendent—the Shepherd-King of God's spiritual nation. David surely was in disfavor with the present king of Israel, but he was close to his King, the Lord God of all.

But David also marveled at how quickly things could change. A secret visit by Jonathan revealed the true depth of Saul's hatred. David panicked. In this moment of crisis, David forgot how the Lord had repeatedly blessed him throughout his life. For a while the songs of faith and praise stopped. David feared for his life. He had no place to hide. His life of comfort and respect in the royal court had fallen apart. So Israel's great hero and champion now fled to Nob, a community of priests that David had visited as Saul's captain of the guard. There a priest named Ahimelech questioned David.

DAVID THE FUGITIVE

To David it sounded as though the priest was suspicious. Acting out of fear and not faith, David responded to his questions with lies. It was an irresponsible act on David's part. Such lies would bring death to this man of God and destruction to his community. David requested food and weapons in order to carry out what he labeled a "special mission of the king." Ahimelech gave him the old loaves of bread from the Lord's table in the tabernacle and offered him the same sword that David had used to slay Goliath.

David craved having the sword: "There is none like it; give it to me!"

Taking the gifts, David continued his flight. But the conversation between David and Ahimelech had been overheard; it would be reported to wrathful King Saul.

Thinking he could hire himself out as a mercenary, David left the hill country of Israel for the coastal plains of the Philistines. He walked into the Philistine city of Gath, the former home of Goliath, and presented himself to Gath's ruler as a mercenary. Some courtiers recognized him. David overheard their whispers: "Isn't he the one they sing about in their dances?"

Suddenly, realizing the danger he was in, David pretended he was insane. He acted like a madman, scribbling marks on the doors and letting drool run down his beard. His behavior made people think he was possessed. The ruler ordered his servants to send David away, out of his court, instead of killing him.

Fleeing the city, David plunged back into the more familiar wilderness of the grazing lands south of Bethlehem, where he occupied a hillside cave.

In the meantime, Saul had interrogated Ahimelech and his companions. He did not believe the honest answers they gave. He ordered his bodyguards to kill all the priests for siding with David. Befriending a lying David had cost Ahimelech his life and the lives of 84 other priests. All were slaughtered on that same day. In fact, every living thing in the community of Nob—men, women, children, and all their animals—met the same sad fate. Nothing was left alive. (Nob in Hebrew means "nothing.") When David learned of this horrible, needless slaughter, he was overwhelmed with guilt.

Ahimelech's son, the only survivor of Nob, fled to David with the high priest's ephod. When he arrived, David immediately acknowledged his sin and confessed his guilt. Then David added: "I am responsible for the death of your father's whole family. Stay with me. The man who is seeking your life is seeking mine also. You will be safe with me." God's forgiveness was evident. Through this man and the ephod, God provided David with personal guidance and answers to his questions.

God also provided companionship and security for David. Men who were distressed, indebted, or discontented came to David. They were willing to fight and die, if necessary, for his cause. His leadership abilities were obvious. He provided for their needs and turned them into a worthy fighting force of four hundred men.

A Chance to Kill the King

God blessed the efforts of David's little army with a victory over Philistine raiders. But Saul soon learned about David's victory.

The Ephod

People have always wanted to know their futures. Some practice astrology. Some turn to soothsayers, fortune-tellers, mediums, and channeling. In ancient cultures people may have slaughtered animals and read the entrails.

God provided his Old Testament people with a means of communicating with him regarding the future. It was the high priest's *ephod*. Worn over linen trousers, a pure linen tunic, and a wide woolen sash, the ephod covered the priest's chest and back. It had a breastplate inset with 12 gemstones and engraved with the names of Israel's 12 tribes. The breastplate was called the *Urim* and *Thummim*—Hebrew words meaning "lights" and "perfections." By contemplating the 12 stones, God would provide the priest with specific answers to important questions.

As New Testament Christians, we, who are all priests of God through Jesus Christ, know that we can talk directly with God in prayer. We also receive guidance through his Word. We have Jesus' assurance that in all things he will work for our good and do what is best.

A five-year game of cat and mouse began.

Saul brought his standing army of three thousand into the hill country in pursuit of David and his followers. David moved east to the oasis at En Gedi and the caves on the shores of the Dead Sea. Saul followed, searching cave by cave through the valley until David was backed into hiding in the inky blackness of one of the caves. Silently, David and several companions crouched in its depths, facing the bright entrance. A hulking, shadowy figure filled the entrance. Saul had them trapped.

But Saul was alone. No soldiers accompanied him. Saul's need to relieve himself had caused him to enter the cave for privacy. Walking into the darkness, he threw off his royal robes, turned, pulled up his tunic, and squatted. As he strained, he had no idea that David and some of his men were hiding in the blackness immediately behind him!

Tempted to take Saul's life, David crept forward, but his conscience would not allow him to strike the king. Instead, he only cut off a corner of the king's discarded robe. When Saul left the cave, David followed him. "My lord the king!" David bowed and prostrated himself with his face to the ground. "This day some urged me to kill you, but I would not lift my hand against the LORD's anointed. See this piece of your robe in my hand. May the LORD vindicate me by delivering me from your hand."

Saul was moved to tears. His conscience had been activated. "You are more righteous than I. You have treated me well, but I have treated you badly. Now swear to me by the LORD that you will not cut off my descendents or wipe out my name from my father's house when you are king." David gave his oath and kept it all his life. Saul returned to his capital, but David remained in the wilderness as a precaution.

To support his followers, David provided protection for the inhabitants of southern Judah from marauding bands of Canaanites. He married a rich widow. Shortly after that, perhaps for political reasons, he took a second wife. God's displeasure with David's decision to disregard the pattern for marriage established at creation is not specifically recorded for us. But there is a record of the discord and disharmony in David's home life as his children would rise up in envy and jealousy against one another and against their father, the king.

Dark thoughts and fears hounded David in the wilderness. "One of these days I will be destroyed by the hand of Saul." Pressure and stress mounted. He was becoming responsible for making decisions for more and more people. He was increasingly busy. There was not enough time! David slipped into a period in his life in which he stopped taking his problems to the Lord and seeking divine guidance through the ephod. Instead, he began to solve problems by himself, saying, "The best thing I can do is to escape to the land of the Philistines. Perhaps then Saul will stop pursuing me."

King Achish received "rebel" David, now the leader of six hundred hardened mercenaries and their families. David asked, "If I have found favor in your eyes, let a place be assigned to me in one of the country towns, that I may live there with our families." That day Achish gave David a distant town in exchange for his services. David presented himself to the king as warring against his own people in southern Judah.

Achish thought that David had become so odious to his own people that he would be an ally forever!

In reality, David was attacking bands of native Canaanite peoples who had not been subdued since the time of Joshua and who continued to terrorize southern Judah with their raids. David's forces would surprise and slaughter everyone—men, women, and children! Not a soul lived to tell what happened! David had become God's hand of judgment!

God's Judgment on the Canaanites

The Canaanites believed that the sexual intercourse of the gods produced rains and bountiful crops. The hilltop worship places were set with sexual asherah poles. Sacred trees were hung with gifts. Temples were sites for male and female prostitution. The Canaanites believed that as the gods watched them, the gods became sexually excited and were intimate themselves. Men trimmed the hair at the corner of their beards for votive offerings fastened to the temple walls. In witness against this practice, God forbade his people to trim the corners of their beards. Jewish men with ringlets in front of their ears still follow this guideline today.

A Canaanite, who chose to devote his life to a goddess, would work himself into a religious frenzy, cut off his genitals, and throw them into the home of his choosing. The occupants, so honored, would respond with gifts of clothing for the new eunuch. The worship of the god Molech, represented with a huge hollow stomach filled with a raging fire, required parents to throw their living children into the fire as sacrifices.

DAVID THE FUGITIVE

God's patience with such people was exhausted. Their time of grace had ended. The annihilation of whole towns was God's righteous judgment being executed at the hands of men like David.

David did not perceive his attacks to be God's righteous judgment. His actions were self-serving. He destroyed all with this justification: "They might inform on us and say, 'This is what David did.'"

For 16 months the pretense worked. Then the Philistines decided to march on Israel! Achish summoned David. "I have found no fault in you. You and your men will accompany me." Achish ordered David's band to form the rear guard of his army. David's "loyalty" would have a real test fighting against Saul and his dearest friend, Jonathan!

However, God moves in mysterious ways. The Philistine captains and other rulers resolved David's problem. "Send the man back, Achish! How better could he regain his master's favor than by taking the heads of our men?" They would not tolerate having David as their rear guard. Achish yielded to pressure and, over David's hollow protests, sent David and his men home.

Military events three days later changed David's life forever. King Saul committed a tactical error. He ordered his army to descend from the heights of the hillsides to fight on the valley floor. But there the Philistines' iron chariots with mounted archers could be used effectively. As the archers got within range, one of them critically wounded Saul. Saul's eldest sons were then killed. Israel was routed, and Saul committed suicide by falling on his own sword.

After pursuing the fleeing Israelites, the Philistines returned the next day to strip the dead. They found the fallen king and his sons. Saul's head was taken as a trophy. His armor was stripped from his body and displayed in the Philistine temples. His naked body, together with those of his sons, was fastened to a wall of the nearby city of Beth Shan.

While this disaster was befalling Israel, David's men picked up the pace as they saw the distant smoke plumes from their village. Their double time broke into a run as they realized the plumes were too large for cooking fires. The members of David's rear guard arrived to find their homes in smoldering ruins. Canaanite raiders had overrun the defenseless town. It looked like one of the towns David's men had destroyed in the past.

Wails tore through the air. Men were wild with grief. David mourned for his family members. Some of the recent recruits directed their anger at David: "Stone him. Stone David! He led us here."

For almost two years, David had tried to solve the nation's problems all by himself. We hear nothing of prayerful songs or psalms of praise during this period. But this total loss, over which he had no control, brought David to his senses and to his knees. A repentant David turned to God.

Summoning Ahimelech's son with the ephod, David asked God: "Shall I pursue this raiding party? Will I overtake them?" And God answered: "Pursue them. You will certainly overtake them and succeed in the rescue."

David's charismatic leadership was evident as he rallied the despairing band that had been ready to stone him. After

DAVID THE FUGITIVE

David spoke, all six hundred took up the pursuit. At dusk they surprised the raiders. In a battle that raged through the night, almost all of the enemies were killed.

What blessing! David and his men rescued every woman and child that had been carried off into slavery. They recovered their possessions and all the plunder the marauders had gathered from neighboring towns. In thanksgiving, David sent gifts back to those Israelite communities that had been raided.

David had learned an important lesson; he was now ready to seek God's help and guidance for the decisions of life.

God led David and his army to Hebron in Judah. There the men of Judah anointed him king, and David ruled Judah for seven years. In David's kingdom, God's will was to be followed.

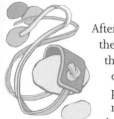

After the death of Saul's surviving son, the elders of the northern tribes of Israel approached David. "In the past, while Saul was king over us, you were the one who led the Israelites on their military campaigns. The Lord said to you, 'You will shepherd my people the Israelites, and you will become their ruler.' Now, be our king." David accepted the invitation and began a 33-year reign over Israel, a united kingdom.

Seeking a neutral site for his capital, David attacked the Canaanite city of Jebus. The Jebusites' stronghold was so well fortified that they bragged, "Even the blind and the lame can ward you off."

Familiar with the city from his shepherding days, David directed the attack through the water shaft, which was used to reach the spring at the bottom of the hill outside the city walls. The strategy was successful. The Jebusite fortress became the City of David. Since it had never been conquered under the judges, it was now the personal property of the king. It is the southernmost hill of the seven hills that make up present-day Jerusalem.

From Jerusalem the united armies of Israel and Judah went forth with God's blessing. David consistently turned to God during these years for guidance and direction. He demonstrated generosity and gracious care and concern toward many, including the surviving members of Saul's household. The Lord was now the complete focus of his devotion, praise, and worship.

The Lord blessed David's reign and made Israel a world power. This tiny kingdom stood at the crossroads of trade between two great world civilizations, Egypt and Mesopotamia.

A Wonderful New Plan

As David gave thanks for his many blessings, a new plan began to take shape in his heart. He said, "It is not right that I should dwell in a house of cedar while the LORD's house is a tent." So David began to think about constructing a marvelous, permanent temple to replace the ancient tabernacle. His stewardship had been blessed with so much silver and gold that it had to be counted by the ton. The gathering of many valuable resources began in preparation for building the Lord's temple.

But God did not allow David to proceed with the building's actual construction. "You are not to build a house for my name, because you are a warrior and have shed blood. Your son will build my house, and I will establish his kingdom forever." God, instead, intended to build a house for David. God's promise looked far beyond the youthful Solomon to a descendant whose kingdom would have no end. The lineage of Jesus Christ, the world's Savior, can be traced legally through Joseph and biologically through his mother, Mary, back to David, the shepherd-king of Israel.

A Sad Chapter in David's Life

The Bible does not make it clear to us why David married multiple wives. The practice of guaranteeing treaties through a king's giving and taking of wives was common. But there was another reason David acquired one of his wives: lust.

Roofs were flat in Palestine. People used their roofs as an

extra room, like a summer porch or a raised deck. One spring evening, when kings should have been with their armies in the field, King David was at home in his palace. The sweet smell of the cedars of Lebanon that paneled his walls filled the air. But he could not sleep. So he went to the rooftop. The east wind had been scorching the city for three days, and everyone was irritable. Perhaps there would be relief from the oppressive heat and the demands of family and office in the cool of the evening. There was no lyre in his hands, no song to the Lord on his lips.

The palace overshadowed all the other houses in the neighborhood. David looked down on his city and saw a woman on her roof. He did not immediately avert his eyes. Idle curiosity slowly became lust as the woman removed her clothes and began to bathe. She was a very beautiful woman. As he watched, David's lust became a raging desire. Who was this woman? He had her identified—Bathsheba, wife of Uriah—and brought to him.

Bathsheba accepted the compliments of the king and acquiesced to his advances. David's frustrations were forgotten as he satisfied his physical desires with her that night. In the morning, David had Bathsheba returned to her home, and he forgot about her.

Busy with affairs of state, David was startled several weeks later when Bathsheba's message arrived: "I am pregnant." The forgotten moment of passion and lust would now consume every waking moment of David's life for the next eight months. This was impossible! Uriah, her husband, a captain in David's army, was away from home, fighting for his king. Bathsheba could not be pregnant!

In panic, David developed a plan to cover the infidelity. "Recall Uriah!"

After a perfunctory review of military action, David told Uriah, "Go down to your wife, and wash your feet." David assumed Uriah would clean up and enjoy being reunited with his wife. The pregnancy would be concealed by Uriah's intercourse with Bathsheba. The child would just be a little premature. No one would even notice the discrepancy.

But Uriah didn't act the way David had expected he would. That night he slept with David's servants and did not go to his wife.

The next morning he explained himself: "The ark and Israel and Judah are staying in tents. How could I go to my house and lie with my wife when my lord's men are in the fields? As surely as you live, I will not do such a thing!"

David got Uriah drunk the next day, but Uriah still refused to enjoy the pleasure of his wife's company while his companions were in danger on the battlefield. David's regimen and code of self-discipline had been thoroughly instilled in his men.

David contrived a second plan. Calling Uriah to him, he gave him a scroll with a secret message for his commander. The message was an order that would place Uriah in harm's way. "Put Uriah in the front line where the fighting is fiercest. Then withdraw from him so he will be struck down and die."

Several days later David's commander obeyed the king's command and placed Uriah under the city wall, where its defenders carried out David's murderous plan.

After the mandatory period of mourning, David brought Bathsheba to his palace as a wife.

David Repents

Trying to hide his sin day after day was devastating for David's faith. David later wrote: "When I kept silent, my bones wasted away through my groaning all day long. For day and night your hand was heavy upon me; my strength was sapped as in the heat of summer."

But God, in his love, reached out to confront David to help him overcome his denial. God sent his prophet Nathan to confront David with his sin.

Nathan told David a story of a callous rich man who took a poor man's only sheep to feed his own guests.

David's anger flared: "Tell me who this is. For this he shall surely die."

Then Nathan pointed the accusing finger directly at David with the words, "You are the man."

Unlike Saul, unlike many, David did not deny, excuse, defend, run, or try to hide. Instead, he confessed his crimes: "I have sinned against the LORD." And in making his confession, David used the special name for his God that meant "my Savior-Friend."

And David was not disappointed in his Savior-Friend's response to his confession.

Nathan now ministered to David, speaking a message about the good news of God's forgiveness. (We call it the gospel.) "The Lord has taken away your sin. You are not going to die. But because you have made the enemies of the Lord show utter contempt, the son born to you will die."

For seven days, David fasted and prayed that God would spare the child's life. But the child did die.

Even the eldest servants were afraid to tell David this sad news. "How can we tell him the child is dead? He may do something desperate!" Seeing them talking in hushed whispers, David asked them to tell him directly what had happened. And they replied, "Yes, the child is dead."

David then amazed his courtiers by getting up, eating, bathing, and going to worship the Lord. He stopped mourning and resumed a normal life. In response to their "Why?" he explained: "While the child was still alive, I fasted and wept. I thought, 'Who knows? The Lord may be gracious to me and let the child live.' But now that he is dead, why should I fast? Can I bring him back again? I will go to him, but he will not return to me." Eternal life and resurrection have been the hope of both Old and New Testament believers. David had that hope . . . for his child, and himself.

David addressed himself to the Lord in a psalm: "Cleanse me with hyssop, and I will be clean. . . . Hide your face from my sins and blot out all my iniquity." He was thinking of the sacrifice that took place on the great Day of Atonement, when a hyssop branch sprinkled the blood of the animal that had been sacrificed on God's altar. This action foreshadowed the events of Calvary, where the sprinkling of Jesus' blood would cover David's sin, and ours.

"O Absalom, My Son!"

The years passed, filled with challenges from the outside and family problems from within. Palace plots and intrigues were common. The lust for power was a constant temptation for those who stood to gain by David's downfall. For a while even one of David's sons, Absalom, managed to wrest power and usurp the throne from his father by siphoning off political and military support for David's rule.

By undermining his father's authority as Israel's legitimate ruler, Absalom's treachery forced David into temporary exile. It was a reluctant father who raised another army to confront his own son, whom he dearly loved. Yet David knew he had a responsibility to govern, for he was God's anointed, the legitimate king of Israel. And even as David waited for a report on the outcome of the battle between his army and Absalom's, David desperately hoped that his son's life might somehow be spared. He had given orders that no one was to harm the young man. But in battle even a king's orders are not always followed.

The battle's outcome was decisive. As Absalom fled from the routing of his defeated army, his thick long hair became entangled in an oak tree. The soldier who discovered Absalom's vulnerability as he hung from the branches of the tree refused to end the usurper's life. He said he would rather obey David's orders and take the chance that Absalom would live on to fight against David's army another day. But one of David's most trusted officers, Joab, dared to disobey the king and put three javelins through Absalom's treacherous heart.

DAVID THE KING

When David learned that his son was dead, he was distraught. "O Absalom, my son, my son," he cried. His heart was broken for his child, who had thoroughly rejected him and his love.

But David's grief for his treasonous son had another unexpected result. David's faithful followers who had just risked their lives to return David to the throne were confused. How could he grieve so for a young man who had just led a rebellion against him? David had to go to extraordinary lengths to win back the hearts of his men and his subjects. His return to Jerusalem to rule the kingdom that was rightfully his had come at a terrible cost—the life of his son.

A Terrible Plague

Near the end of his life, a sinful pride seized David's heart. He decided to take a census to confirm his success. Advisers recognized the wrong motivation for David's action, but the king was adamant and ignored sound advice. It took nine months, but the report was presented to the aged king. "You command 1.3 million men ready and fit to wield the sword."

This knowledge did not bring pleasure. Sinful knowledge and sinful actions do not bring satisfaction. Either they lead to a desire for greater satisfaction and more sin or one's conscience is awakened. In David's case, it was the latter. David confessed to the prophet Gad, "I have sinned greatly in what I have done."

Again David's forgiveness was complete, but David and the people of his kingdom would experience a chastisement—a loving lesson from God.

God sent his prophet Gad to David with three choices: three years of famine, three months of fleeing from your enemies, or three days of plague in the land. A repentant David now placed himself entirely into God's loving hands, choosing three days of plague.

By the third day, the plague had spread across the land and the angel of the Lord was at the threshing floor on the hill directly north of Jerusalem. This hill had been the site of the proposed sacrifice of Isaac by Abraham centuries before. It would be the site of the temple of Solomon, and later Herod's temple. David's prayer in this time of national crisis foreshadowed the actions and prayers of the Good Shepherd, who would one day sacrifice his life for the sake of his flock. "These are but sheep. What have they done? Let your hand fall upon me."

God answered David through the prophet: "Go up, and build the altar." And David did just that, buying the land, oxen, and wood from the landowner.

That very day the plague ended. The world was given another picture of what would happen through Jesus, the future son of David. Just as a ram was substituted at that hill for Isaac and David's sacrifice was accepted there for the people, so the centuries' sacrifices would be accepted there, at the temple, in the place of the nation's sin. Finally, the perfect sacrifice for sin, the lifeblood of the innocent Lamb of God, would be given in that very place to cover sin for all eternity.

Why is so much of the biblical record devoted to the life of David? And why are his many years of successful rule, filled with blessings for the nation, ignored in the Bible account, only to spend long chapters on David's moments of personal failure?

David was a man of repentance. When he looked in the law of God and saw the ugliness of his sin, David was sincerely sorry. But he also understood and believed God's promise of forgiveness. On the great Day of Atonement, David trusted that the hyssop branch covering the mercy seat of the ark with the sacrificial lamb's blood assured him of God's forgiveness. "Purge me with hyssop and I will be clean," was David's confidence. He listened to the pronouncement of complete forgiveness and believed the Lord God with all his heart. He studied God's Word for guidance in his life and talked with his Lord frequently in prayer. He surrounded himself with Christian advisors and listened to their counsel. He chose and implemented new God-pleasing courses of action. He practiced his faith openly, engaging in personal acts of bravery, graciousness, and generosity. He left an inspired witness to his faith in his psalms, which God has preserved for us so that we too might receive blessing through David, the shepherd-king of Israel.